Dominic Berry is the host of **POETS AND MASH**, a celebration of Manchester's rising poetry stars, last Monday every month at Matt and Phred's, Tib St. He also co-hosts **FREED UP** (the only open mic in town where you get free cake) at greenroom theatre, third Thursday each month. September 2008 saw the birth of **ANIMAL WRITES**, a social group for animal lovers who want to share poetry or prose (though not necessarily about animals!) in Manchester's 8th Day Cafe. Firmly established as Manchester's Queer Vegan Poet, Dominic is always gigging somewhere, so check www.myspace.com/thepoetdominic for updates on where he's up next. You can contact him at thepoetdominic@hotmail.co.uk.

Hey Richard

Thanks for cheering us on!

Dominic

First published in 2008 by
Flapjack Press
6 Chiffon Way, Trinity Riverside, Gtr Manchester M3 6AB
www.mucusart.co.uk/flapjack.htm

Printed in Great Britain by
www.printondemand-worldwide.com

ISBN-13 978 0 9555092 2 3

Versions of **Solid with Stardust** appeared in *The Mental Virus, The Ugly Tree* & *Sticks and Stones*; versions of **The Road To Trefasser (Part 1)** & **Kebab** appeared in *The Mental Virus*; versions of **Lovely Fruit Salad** appeared in *The Vegan* & 8th Day's *Delia, Schmelia*; versions of **My Favourite Meals**, **Green as The Fields** & **Beers in Your Bedroom** appeared in 8th Day's *Delia, Schmelia*; a version of **I'm Coming Out as Vegan!** appeared in *T.O.F.U.*; **Night in July** appeared in Commonword's *Pipeline*; **Do You See This Night?** & **Sits with Buddleia** appeared in *The Ugly Tree*; **Stranger Dress** & **Sellotape Smile** appear in Route's *Foreword* collection.

Cheers to Gerry, Brink, Rod, Rachael, Steve O and Richard Weeden for all your invaluable feedback and to Niven, Graeme and Upekshapriya for doing my YouTube stuff. Thanks to my family for all their endless support. Top banana to Shabina, Cheryl, Hannah, John and all at Contact who helped me create *'Lovely Fruit Salad'*. 2 up thumbs to David Hoyle, Libby at Central Library, Ann at Apples & Snakes, Liz and PANDA, Commonword, Write Out Loud, CAN, LiveAMP, VADA, Queer Up North, Poetica, Speakeasy, Shangri La's, Don't Miss This, Taurus, 8th Day, Vegan Society, Royal Exchange, Matt and Phred's, greenroom and all who support me staging my work. Aubergines all round!

Dominic Berry

TOMORROW, I WILL GO DANCING

Flapjack press

CONTENTS

MY FAVOURITE MEALS

TOMORROW, I WILL GO DANCING

INTRODUCTION

Escaping Welsh valleys meant I could begin to heal from having lived in Welsh valleys.

Manchester. Gave me Chloe Poems. Rosie Lugosi. Lemn Sissay. James Quinn.

Being quite a gloomy fellow (in my black mini-skirt and steel toe-capped boots), I began sharing my quite gloomy verse out and about on Manchester's glorious poetry scene. I knew what my beer was for.

Then, in 2007, I got a wonderful residency at the healing hub that is Contact Theatre and was inspired to create a Performance Poetry nightclub, *'Lovely Fruit Salad'*. For the first time, I wrote about love.

Love for fruits.

Love for Battle Wagon (my first bike). Love for a plastic action toy called Beast Man. Love for my Manchester (a double brunchfast in Mod Pop Café, then over to Greenhouse for those great new vegan doughnuts). Love for Sale Water Park and Cafe Ark. Love for my gloomy poems. Love for people (and when I say people, I refer to Benjamin Zephaniah's poem and quote "Cows are people too"). Love for me. Love and incomparable respect for my single Mum's fantastic strength, not only in surviving Thatcher's Cruel Britannia, but also in empowering me with politics, passion and poetry.

But, above all else, I wrote my love for dancing. Really camp dancing.

Love for shaking my groove thang. Love for the red shoes. Love for dancing to the end of love, dancing in the street (my favourite song ever. Martha Reeves, I love you!).

Before poems, before words, was there any purer way of expressing total joy than dancing? Yet, in a society determined to celebrate violence and thuggery, dancing can be difficult.

Sometimes, when people hear me read *'Trying to Remember'*, they come up after and say, "That must be a really old poem, there's no homophobia these days."

I'm surprised they can see me, as they're obviously blind.

Being beat up is awful. People can thump you, physically and mentally, and know they won't get challenged. The police don't stop it, our MPs won't stop it, everyone's too scared. We're even scared of kids. But that mustn't stop us dancing. When we are out dancing, we know they haven't won.

> *"Love the imperfect*
> *Rejoice in the unconventional*
> *Everything that is different*
> *Embrace it as your own*
> *and hold it close to your heart*
> *Take time to explore and reflect*
> *Wonder at diversity*
> *Be inspired*
> *and be yourself."*
> Karen McCloud

There is so much in life to celebrate. These pages celebrate stuff that is dear to me. I'm so happy to see my first collection of big, gay, vegan poems being published.

So happy, I'm gonna go dancing.

Dominic ✖

ENTRÉE

Once, a long time ago, this young man was even younger. I remember it as if it were yesterday: Dominic Berry bounded onto the stage of *Slam Bam Thank You Ma'am*, a poetry event run by my alter ego Chloe Poems. Dominic's entrance was not just accompanied by his poem but also by his underpants. Just him, his poem and his underpants; it was an event in itself. It was most definitely a splash, resulting in Chloe baptising him the best bottom in British poetry. I don't know if Dominic's bottom has grown more rounded and substantial but his poetry most certainly has. Dominic's typically vivacious debut resulted in a colourful and dramatic series of stage personas. From cyber goth to gutter drag, Dominic has flavoured his performances with the vivacity of vaudeville and the integrity of a wordsmith. His regular appearance at Chloe's slams gave me the opportunity to see this very different voice blossom and bloom. I've made Dominic sound a little bit showbiz methinks, but that would do this bold and very real writer's work a disservice.

There is a commitment to this poet's material that comes from both the necessity to write and also the desire to make that writing vital and organic. Dominic isn't afraid of poetics. Although urban, Dominic also enjoys the urbane. There's as much here about the horrors and delights of city nights as there is about cake. From the warmth and inconsistencies of family life to the deconstruction of self through the reconstruction of sexuality, Dominic diverts and distracts with equal pleasure. This isn't just an autobiographical journey through his life, but a dodgem car ride through bits of our own.

I've had the joy of working with Dominic, both as a performer and mentor, and have admired the commitment he puts equally into his writing and performances. Dominic can act, sing, direct, lead workshops and dance, but for me his greatest strength is in being a performance poet. When I say that, I mean he is both a fine performer and exceptional writer. For me, a true performance poet has to have these qualities in abundance.

I believe this collection will help solidify this already established performer and allow his work to travel further than ever before. The smell of youth permeates this book like a slow-rising sponge and is accompanied by the emergence of a confident and accomplished young man: a Dominic cake. Think of it as a smorgasbord of terribly satisfying nibbles. A well-pinched selection of hard and soft centres, a picnic at the most picturesque spot you can imagine or just a lovely fruit salad.

I am confident that this book will be the first course of many. Compliments to the chef.

Gerry Potter

This book's dedicated to all the poets I've met who've given
me inspiration and shared their spark.
Far too many to mention. You know who you are!

FROM BEDDINGTON AND CARSHALTON

Mother and rising son
alone.
Thatched Britain burning.
It's a witch hunt.
Mum is single minded. She will protect
with not even a broom stick to call her sword.
Me, I'm a baby goblin,
warm blooded reptile with a lion's tail.

Those who were friends would now watch us burn.
Watching, whispering,
"Dirty girl."
"Yeah," she smiles back.
"Dirty."

I marvel Mum's strength. Solid with stardust.
Woman powered beyond comprehension
shows me life's sparks. Dark, mystic arts.
Lizards and butterflies ink dance her skin.
Flower fairies leap in bedraggled glamour.
Eyes speak of wardrobes that all lead to Narnia,
sweet and sour truths brewed by midnight
candle light, cauldron deep.

A witch's familiar,
this black cat's tight round Mum's ankles.
She's always been proud
when the good people have come down,
crucifixes in hand,
preparing our bonfire.

If she had died, then she would have been human

but I know she is super natural.
Love will lead me,
spellbound.

DIAMONDS

We are ring without stone.
Rich belong to rich.
Diamonds are mean,
clean jewels for tidy, shiny families.
Diamonds, a boy's worst friend.
They're forever.
Aren't they?
Reminding what will never be.
Lingering fingers flaunt sharp rocks.
Always pointing.

DON'T BANK LOVE

Our love
in shoe boxes under the bed,
in brown, big envelopes
stuffed,
loaded
under the armchair.

Banks give plastic.
Don't see or feel.
Accept transaction
without question.

Our home
takes love with one sugar.
Stuffed,
loaded
sprawls through woodchip.

Boys love bikes.
I hate mine.
Stabilisers taken,
Mum and her cuddles inside as
clumsy Step Dad holds my saddle,
runs close. I pedal.
Don't let go!

Down a back alley street, so far from my pillow,
handlebars jiggle under sweat wet palms.
Spokes growl grumble. Belly drum rumbles.
Feet cartwheel like bumbling clowns
on Big Top's opening night.
Propelled by fright, I glance back to see him
laugh at me.
He's let go.

I fumble. Teeter.
Clumsy me!
No safety net beneath trapeze.
He laughs

then I laugh too.
Ha!
I let go.
Woah!
Crack through air like ring master's whip.
Phased.
Amazed.
Shot free of my cannon. Rocket and fly!
Tear through skies whose horizons had fallen
down the back of a hug.

Mum might be cooking.
I feast on speed.
My tummy, a circus.

THIS
IS
HOME

THE ROAD TO TREFASSER (PART 1)

Crawling with confidence like mumbling tractors,
faces ploughed barren, furrowed scowls.
No trust in these wrinkles, only suspicion.
Boot soles mucky with cow shit and tradition.
"Gays should be shot."

This farmyard sleeps with one eye open.

Hills litter threats and rumours.
Slap chunks of wood in open fists.

Join Mum.
Big, new settee.
Play Guns and Roses.
Anarchy, peanut butter toasted.
Bet she misses the city paradise.
Sing
"So far away. So far, far away . . ."

With great bleeding badges carved in grubby knees
boys outside are climbing trees.
I build cities, my toys explore.

My Step Dad hates action men.
Clumsy man, always sorry,
words won't fit his mouth.
He does gardens. Fucking trees.
I scratch poems on their dead insides,
make paper cloaks for my Warrior Witch,
as rain chuckles gutters outside

home.

A breath stealing country. Mountains piled high.
"Come out, poof . . ." carved in the sky.
Sunset colour of crumbling brick.
Cattle beaten with labourer's stick.
Farmyard boys, knuckles like bark
"We'll punch your lights out after dark."
Cows kept under barn and key
locked in terminal greenery

and Axel Rose
and Evil Lyn
cuddled up tonight

oppose the system
munching toast
on the big, new settee.

HOME OF BEASTS

Beetled walls protect
our woodloused floors, our spidered
roof, our great small lives.

BEAST

Firm body.
Squishy head.
Nearly nude in plastic fur trunks.

Some toys have removable armour.
I draw hairs on their bare chests.

Then Beast Man came
with hair.
Yeah.
His rage strong face perfect in hate.
Huge weapon (thicker than his arm!)
plotting thrill in a city I create.
Dominic's demonic Malt Wheatie box castle
taped to evil toilet roll turrets.

In a shoe box dungeon, Beast Man want orgy.
Unclip armour.
"Filthy queer."
He rams Fisto,
fists Ram Man,
says *"Skeletor has a hairy arse."*

Bum him, Beast Man, bum him good!
Make him bend with pipe cleaner whips.

Smooth, blonde goodies are boring
like morals.
Like mortals.
Wet as paint that never dries.
Smaller weapons. Bland, hairless chests.
Clueless with maidens (who always get captured).
Women are better stood on their own.

Tough girls, Warrior Goddesses,
not skinny blubbers who wail *"Help me!"*
to clumsy heroes,
action free.

My hairy baddy buddy is tough.
Rough.
Mind power mage with mane of fire.
Leave the girls.
Kidnap me.
I won't wail, whatever you do.

Kill the klutz trying to rescue me.
Stab your flame blade, snap his shield,
spill goodie goodie gut drops.
Splatter splutter drool and pool.

Pinch me.
Cackle in my face.
Hook my naked breath on your sword.
Squishy body.
Firm head.
Carve chest burn skin curls.
Rip my thighs.

I'm brave.
Let's touch you.
Feel real hair.
I can be beast.

NO CAT

Nippy is not a cat.
He's the Pembrokeshire Panther,
Trefasser his Malay Peninsula,
hunting voles and torn bits of leaf.

Nippy's no cat.
He is sky on ground.
His grey hairs glimmer,
dots of star in rolling black galaxy.
Jumps to kitchen window ledge,
a big bang.
Beams down for tea,
"How'd he get behind you?"
then he's up on the worktop,
paws in your food!
It's Star Trek at 6 on BBC 2,
then back, boldy out, to explore.

Nippy's no cat.
He is Grace Jones.
Your feet are Russell Harty.
Claws and flat-eared battle cries wait
coiled back between telly and sofa.
Unsocked ankles,
beware!

Nippy's no cat.
He is Godzilla, Kit Kong,
that cat in The Goodies.
Belly crashes down upon towns of Lego
I build for him to destroy.

Nippy's no cat.
He is *"The Most Powerful Man In The Universe!"*

Humbles He Man. Never a Cringer.
Squeezing through Castle Grayskull's jaw bridge,
purrs and pummels keep Evils at bay.
Hurray!
We saved the world today.
Up to the jersey on my bed for a quick nap and dribble.
We snooze in celebration before our foes regroup.

Nippy's no cat.
He's a warlock's close spirit. Telepathic muse
walks widdershins behind the chicken shed,
chats silent under tree shadow.
We share marmite sandwiches, ketchup flavoured crisps.
Only he gets me outside myself,
confiding the nothings of school,
the everythings of tomorrow.

Nippy listens.
"Prrrrrrrrr."
We make maps out of twigs.

BEAUTIFUL BEAUTIFUL
for a girl I knew on the pebble beach

She lets me in her white wine dress.
I'm barefoot in the stream.
For school breaks. Summer bakes
the gorse and blue berry.
We're singing on a pebble beach.
I can hear lambs bleat
in fields on hills that hug our bay,
lay drinking in the heat.
So keep the boys and balls about
a hundred cliffs from me.
For school breaks. Those boys would take
this beautiful, beautiful dream.
Can I keep it?
If I can keep it, keep me in
this beautiful dream.

Boys once tore her white wine dress.
She won't let them tear me.
Barefoot in rock pools
sheltered from the sea.
Waves applaud my summer song.
We're so alive and free.
She holds me in her white wine dress
delicate and clean.
Tells me I look beautiful.
Waves and stone agree.
I love her. She is not alone
inside this beautiful dream.
Let's keep it.
If we can keep it, keep us in,
this beautiful dream.

Clasped inside her white wine dress
and tears from where she's been.
The city stink of boys and balls
where blood ran down her knee.
For school breaks. Her joy aches,
complete by holding me
in fields on hills. No city stink.
We're somewhere nice and green.
Don't want to want the boys or balls
a hundred cliffs from me.
Want to love the dress I'm loved inside.
This beautiful dream.
She can keep me
if she can keep me.
If she can keep me, please keep me in
this beautiful, beautiful dream.

JOCELYN AND COHEN DUET

I DJ for daddy long legs.
They flump through air like first time drunks
to *'Somebody Else's Guy'*.

Jocelyn Brown
boom-ba-booms my walls,
spills out window cracks,
fills Pen Caer's starved valleys.

Pause the cassette.
Search bedroom for *'Tower of Song'*.
Find CD
shining under Dungeons and Drag Queens.
Wipe my sword and record.
I'm a remixed hero.

In my eyes . . . this is London's Heaven!
Imagine me, steamed up in molten synth,
sizzle braised in capital city.

Bet all night clubbers love Leonard Cohen
deep disco,
poetry raves and friends.

First, I'll take Pembrokeshire
then, I'll take the Thames.

FUCK ME, LONDON

Hey. London.
Fuck me, London.

I'm here on a trip. Please, take grip.
Ride our car, topless,
bare back seat, rip our roof wide,
shoot your London spurt inside.
Fuck me alive. I came dead.
Fuck London breath into my head.
Remind me how to breathe,
throat deep.
Never sleep.
Never weep.

Fuck me, screaming. Fuck me, dumb.
Fuck me, London, then fuck my Mum.

Yes! Mum. Fuck. We can swear here.
Bold queer. No fear.

Imagine divorcing my Step Dad, Mum,
then you'd always feel like this.
London fucking you! London fucking me!
London, smokey fit.
Let's stay. Be gay!
Cramped crowd stiff.
Graffiti smacked on barest brick.
Polluted mouths. Fucking loud!
Gimme the keys. Mum, please
don't take us home to the cruel country.

Marc Bolan was killed by a tree.

Let me *be* fuck . . . like Freddie Mercury!

Acid served by naked dwarves.
Mum, aren't these things you applaud?
Aren't you stardust? T-Rex gold?
Don't let marriage turn you old.

That wedding ring's a circle of hate.
Let London fuck us, Mum. Don't wait.
That wedding ring is a circle of fear.

Bet my real Dad's fucking here.

BEETROOT JUICE

Say it in a mirror 3 times.
I met a man with snake hair,
merry-go-round tongue,
he heart haunts me from beneath the sand.

Love is to live in 2 worlds at once.
As my hand writes, without him,
I hear my feet in another realm
dancing up fire as he slaps his drum.

I used to hate beetroot.
Was told it was *"good"*,
like *"lettuce"* and *"marriage"*
(stuff other people pushed on my plate).
Knew I wasn't good.
Even before my desires were unearthed
Beetroot knew I was bad.
"Boys who want boys go to hell."

Beetroot Juice
Beetroot Juice
Beetroot Juice

Staining lips. Smeared on cheeks.
Call this sin?
Count me in.
Flavours in my mouth unsealed.
Favours in the beetroot fields.
Roasted. Grated. Diced. Peeled.
He revealed my dream denied,
guilt fear cast aside,
ripped open wide, burst free.

Call this hell?
Well
I pray I never leave.

Hold me in his ecstasy.
Sucking beetroot.
He and me.

MEN IN SUITS, BOYS IN SCHOOL UNIFORM

Did not drown.
Drowned a dream.
Dreamt I would conform
like men in suits. Boys in school uniform.

Dreamt of how
I'd march through life,
proudly wear clothes men have worn,
men in suits. Boys in school uniform.

Tight, white clothes can disguise
in handsome shades of truth
what kills or cripples youth.
Their hearts look smart.
They're smart. Not warm.
Men in suits. Boys in school uniform.

Did not drown.
I drowned a dream of dressing in their style
once I learned I never would,
never could, not while
what filled their hearts would tear and gash.
Viciously fighting for designer trash!
To covert and claw,
aching to own just a little bit more.
Heard the sound of a shirt getting torn.
Men in suits. Boys in school uniform.

So, stripped
down to my swimming trunks!
Derobed desire of trendy junk.
Competitive greed now defunct.
Dived in water, clean and free,
able to see

my confidence was far from shrunk.
Rose like Neptune, pierced and punk!
Thrust my trident far and near.
Blast my conch shell down your ear.
"Did not drown!"
Make that clear.

I drowned a dream.
I'm still here.

Didn't say *"I love you"*
after our first kiss.
Waited 'til our first wank

then mid-spank, blurted, *"Babe,*
I will always worship your boner,
always savour your cologne and
everytime you leave home, I will
always track where you're goin' ta
like bats do with sonar.
I'll keep messaging your phone,
never let you be alone.
Will text ya 'til my thumbs drop off,
'til the day I die!"

and he said *"Goodbye."*

I said, *"Well, fuck you, you . . . fuck."*
then left, bereft.

My first love. A hero.
Would've been his Lois Lane.
When I picture his super arse I think
"I'll never wash this tongue again."

Thought love was an everlasting gobstopper.
Mine was more like a tic tac.
Well now I'm off to stuff my face.
I'm never coming back.

No, I'm not goin' to Uni.
Working ain't for me.
I'm going on the dole
and I'll fuck every man I see!

Gonna out-shag Casanova.
Come on, Mum. Don't cry.
My whole life's just one word away.
That word is *"Goodbye."*

MANCHESTER

City of living myth
can breathe legend to chimney smoke.
Beckons fire.
"You can dance . . . for inspiration!"
Perspire.
Hotter than internet hackers,
E'd up Uni slackers,
that lovely Shayne Ward's naked knackers
or even Bez's sweaty maracas.

Hot as invisible sky beast
made of promises, verse and beat.
Whispers, *"Won't let you down.*
Let's show you round town."

Winged.
Smouldering heart.
Pulse under skin of leathered scallies.
Great Brutish beauty grips with talons
that smell of chip paper and wow.
"Get hold o' this"

and up
and up
and up

vapour trail past Portland Street,
cling to steam sodden claw.
Soar, wind snapping hair,
higher than the Hilton,
breathing stars.
Then, dip down to Daleks
singing *"Y.M.C.A."*

Lazers and plungers raised
in Fab Café!
But don't stay. Rip away!
Too swift and sly.
So dive into darker
Shag-tag-ular dares.
"Pinch Brian Molko's kiss
from the top of Affleck's stairs."
Then, in a muggy, crowded daze,
taste thin lines of silver in moist, clouded haze.
See poems, rain bathing, in paving cracks and wall.
Where bass lines rise, boxer shorts fall.
Hear curried conversation, soft canal call,
backstreeting, drum beating, drunk caterwaul

and down.

Dropped off at the anywhere
stomachs unload.
Cock-a-doodle students
are spilling out jeans all up Oxford Road.
Belts hover round white briefed buttock.
Gravity defying pants.
I wanna be the serpent
when that one's apples drop.

Gathering up eyeballs
I show him some teeth,
belt loop his thumbs,
whisper *"Won't let you down.*
Let's ride.
I know where this city has wings."

I KNOW WHAT MY BEER IS FOR

NIGHT IN JULY

Night in July. Town is dead.
Trains come and go through the station.
From my platform I feel myself hurry down.
I unzip with appropriate hesitation.
A pin-stripe man with his briefcase leaves
the toilets lying empty and my heart fills my gut, so
I think about trains. Imagine destinations
while my dick stays wrinkled and my thighs tight shut and
I don't go home on a night in July.
When town is dead I am grateful.

Mum made me roast almost every night.
I'd eat what was given. I'm not wasteful.
We'd talk about work. I'd love what we'd do.
I do what I'm told. I am grateful.
But now I'm not home. Now, my fingers stink of piss.
The air smells of shit. I am shaking at the wrist.
I am not going home. Stood here alone.
Think of roast dinners. Think what I've missed.
Think about trains, Mum and home.
Think what I've missed. I am grateful.

Night in July. I close my eyes.
Think about platforms. Imagine situations.
Imagine the man. Pin-striped. Briefcased.
Trains tug their load through the station.
He says *"Love what we do. Do what you're told."*
and every ache place I feel his kiss,
his touch, his breath, his eyes; I'm scared but
my mouth tastes of him and my fingers smell of his
and I roast in his warmth. Imagine destinations.
Stood here alone. I am grateful.

I open my eyes. Night in July.
The briefcase man in pin-stripe *is* behind me.
He unzips himself with appropriate hesitation,
shaking at the wrist as his hand moves to find me.
I . . . run for my platform, doors close behind me,
train home alone, I do what I'm told.
Where my mouth tastes of nothing and my fingers don't stink.
Don't even want Mum to love and hold.
My dick pressed down and my thighs tight shut.
Night in July. I am grateful.

RETAIL WHORE

Retail People grind in wedlock.
Monogamous workloads ring them dry.

Why?

I flirt, flit, to work won't commit,
let them shaft me casually
but we all know employers can't stand a slut.

They say, *"Brief affairs
are such immature behaviour"*
though I have no cares
while they're married to their labour.

They say, *"Brief affairs
sour how our Bosses rate us"*
but their lives aren't theirs.
They're existing for status.

I'm a Retail Whore,
had more jobs than they've hot dinners.
Aren't our lives worth more,
or is independence saved for sinners?

FIVE RHYTHMS

The body tips, pours
slipshod through rigid air like
magma through glacier.

Feet stab up a storm
whilst wrists slice and whiplash,
strip chunks off of breath.

Pulse of a tempest
where hearts can upturn ships, sweat
the salts out the sea.

Roar into these shores,
curl like wave's crest, crack and rip
wet from opened lips.

Now, lap against the
break of cool arms. Tide turns and
leaves life in rock pools.

NIGHT IN AUGUST

Hanging round beer thick crowds.
One sharp lad hooks my eye.
Bleach blonde spikes. Grubby Nikes.
Ice white vest in August twilight.
Combat pants with button down fly
loosely grip skinny hips.
Grinning at me, warm and pally,
beckons me up a dirt darkened alley.
I smile, follow, then smile again
outside a public convenience
for gentlemen.

Glory holy temple of bleached methane
burns my nose but fires the mind!
His fly's unbuttoned. Bulging. Begging.
Alien lap burster!
Thirsty to be drunk.
Lick my fingers like sherbet dippers.
Slide them under elastic rimmed boxers.
Cottoned crotch. Warm, wet creases.
Clammy thighs. A sticky feast. His
pubic hair, goose bump raised,
spiky hard. Recently shaved.

Push him round. Shorts pulled down.
Whip cream tasty. Soft shaky.
Jonny tugged tight in disinfectant wreak.
Push in hard. Push in deep.
Push in prickling short trimmed hair.
A jagged gasp. *"Fuck, yeah!"*
His legs tremble. Mine are steel.
Inside my cock's a Catherine wheel.
His buttocks grip tighter than if
he hung from a cliff held only to my dick.

Fingers dig in side of ribs.
Gritting teeth climax spits.

Hits the spot.
Bull's-eye shot.
Shit hot.

Silently drag up pants.
I leave him first.
"..."
Relax.

TINY BUTCH

I know. I need you less than I choose.
I'm out on the street where you bribe with abuse.
Your body got blunt, wore down through overuse.
Hello, Tiny Butch. It's the same old news.

But now, I know I've nothing that attracts you anymore.
I am camp, I am fat and you've fucked me before
and I have no use while I'm still sore.
I'm no use, not while your

body is a battle. You are tiny, Butch. Too active.
You're full. You are full. You empty. Fill and empty.
You have emptied me to fill me and you've filled me 'til I'm empty,
'til I know that I have nothing that attracts you anymore.
I am camp, I am fat and you've fucked me before.

But I'm no Tiny Butch! Well, you won't feed
on a camp, fat blubber who won't bend and bleed,
on a camp, fat blubber embarrassed by greed,
on a camp, fat blubber who trusted. Believed.

So now I choose to have you less in my life than I chose.
I am no Tiny Butch. I've grown out your clothes
and I have no use for your cheap blows.
I've no use, not while those

bodies are in battle. Tiny. Butch. Active.
Fill. Fill. Fill! Empty. Fill and empty.
You won't empty me to fill me. You won't fill me 'til I'm empty,
'til I'm empty, full and empty and feel nothing anymore,
'til I'm camp, fat and hungry and feel nothing anymore,
'til I think that I am nothing when I'm hungry, when I feed,

so, I choose to have you less
than I need.

I KNOW WHAT MY BEER IS FOR

I know what my beer is for.
Try hard to forget these ways
but I know what my tears are for.
No one keeps forever these days.
I know there is no true love
a better flesh won't soon upturn.
I know there is no true love.
It's with my beer I come to learn.

But . . . I can't
get used to temporary stability
with one who feels like iron,
then melts before the third degree.
So, hold me.
Fool me. Craft a lie that I can't see.
So skillfully weave
that for one moment I believe.

Because I know what your leers are for,
to hook me up with fuck me eyes,
and I know what my fears are for
I jump before the lies capsize.
Because I know there is no true love!
Sweet deceit pricks the sore.
I know there is no true love
because I know what my beer is for.

But . . . I can't
get used to temporary stability.
Must do. Try to
fake a little faith, so you
can hold me.
Bruise me. Use me. I'm your commodity.
I will fool myself for this,
if you give me one moment
blind by bliss.

GAY PARADE

Smiled up in this thick parade, he
put my pint glass on the ground.
Sunk an arm into my thigh.
Glitter spat where we sat down.
Kissing disco drenched his skin.
Honey coloured. 'lectro light.
Buttocks like two slabs of marble.
Sequinned rainbow banners slashed the night.

He said, *"Our lovers are our family.*
All are loved and loving loud.
As a child I only dreamt
of being this carefree and proud.
I can hold my father's words,
then rip them up and dance away.
Sea of tongue. Suede head leather.
Glistening thoughts that warm me through the day."

I wiped my lips, said, *"Yes, they're loud*
and yeah, they'll love, but soon ignore,
avoid or tread on those who've given
what they've got and have no more.
Carefree men with hollow smiles
don't have any care to bring,
just endless unremembered names
and banners that could say anything."

We paused. He stood, said, *"Fair enough,*
I guess you'll not come back again"
then rejoined the crashing crowd,
a grinning pool of liquid men.
Tidal wave of salty chests,
Cheekbones aimed, hands raised high.
Picked my pint up. Sat and drank.
Camp loud laughter built. Blurred the sky.

FANTASTIC

Hey! My wrists are healing well.
She kissed me and she said,
"Let's do it on the patio.
We don't need the shed."
She even loves these petrol burns
where my stomach bled.
No more toilet cubicles.
We touch in my own bed

'cos everything's fantastic now.
It took so long to say
but everything's amazing since I said
"I'm not gay!"
I've never been so happy.
She will never go away.
Folk'll cope without us
if we stay in bed all day.

She said: *"Let's get some goldfish,*
no more pigeons like he owns.
Now, if you get a bus at night
you won't get hit by stones.
Now, if you call your Dad, you might
hear more than dialling tones.
Now if you find a real love,
love won't be lent in loans."

Oh, everything's fantastic now.
It took so long to say,
but everything's been fabulous
since I've not swung that way.
I've never felt so happy.
Please don't go away.
Folk'll cope without us
if we stay in bed all day

and I would rather spend my life in bed
than be an easy lay.

NOT MY FATHER

Tomorrow, I'll go dancing
because I am not my father.

Buying books on How to Breathe
because I am not my father.

Buggered at Goodwick Youth Club
because I am not my father.

We're there, so fun at weekends
because I am not my father.

Read Six Women Poets on a cliff edge at night
because I am not my father.

You'll have to come back in the morning
because I am not my father.

I'm sorry Mum
because I am not my father.

Sometimes I'm a bit Elaine Paige
because I am not my father.

A pin-stripe man with his briefcase leaves
because I am not my father.

Yes, I do like being violent
because I am not my father.

Never say I love you
because I am not my father.

I would take a bullet
because I am not my father.

Call me any name you like
because I am not my father.

Call it *"the little death"*
because I am not my father.

Tell me I won't leave you
because I am not my father.

Can't let this poem stop
because I am not my father.

KEBAB

My love for you won't falter.
Can't ease without you in me.
Come on, now,
soothe this aching, sleepless dream.

Get me
on my feet. Back home.
Just past the tightening dancers.
Where every screw's a life that could have been.

Get me
warm. Safe from harm.
Greasy calm. Send me,
like bedtime fairy stories Mum would read.
A little treat of something's all I need.

You say; *"Love.*
Don't be sad and empty.
Breathe my heat.
Press your lips to me.
I'll bite your tongue.
Spice in your saliva.
Hot cha cha!
I clog up all your feeling."

You block up all my senses.
A hug that's like an anchor
pulls me to the closest bed I found.
Under sheets, like hiding underground.
Hear the night. Just a distant sound
of stupid dancers screaming, *"It's your round!"*
Car alarms and hen parties are drowned.
I'm all right
'til tomorrow night

then once again the queen will get de-crowned,
and I'll be at the kebab counter, counting pound on pound

to buy your love.
I am not sad and empty.
Bring me love.
I'll ease with you in me.
Bring me love
or clog up all my feeling.
No alarm
clogging up my feeling.
Safe from harm.
Clogging all my feeling
'til I'm gone.

MY FAVOURITE MEALS

THE HAPPIEST MEAL

Don't you live on TV?
Ronald! You are a man.
Do you have a willy?
Are you American,
like dinosaurs or Santa Claus?
Do you know Moschops?
Is this where your hamburgers grow
from seeds off of burger bun tops?

If you ate the burger seeds,
would a tree grow inside you?
Would branches poke out of your nose,
covered in bogey goo?
Then, would they grow snot burgers
that taste of burger and snot?
Would the tree get bigger and bigger
inside you until you went 'pop'!

Y'know your burger friends, that talk,
do you eat them as well?
What if a speaking one's fallen asleep
and you've eaten him - how can you tell?

Wow! A crown! Balloons and toys!
Ronald, you give so much to boys.
You're like Michael Jackson
          but white.   ·
Do you have a son?
Do you eat burgers every night?

Do you stay up after bedtime, hidden
where the burgers grow?
I bet you get away with loads
and no one tells you no!

D'you teach your son to grow his food
from the burger seed?
Do you read him fairy stories
then clap 'cos you believe?

Do you do each other's lipstick?
Will he be on telly too?
I wish you could be my Dad, Ronald.
I've learned loads from you.

GREEN AS THE FIELDS

See a farmyard hen,
inquisitive, friendly.
Not a cute kitten or puppy.
All her summers sunny side up.
See her, scratching for a seed in this head,
scraping brain soil with dinosaur feet.
She excavates images,
scrabbles through skull's earth,
muddied burger bites and birthday treat.
Claws up crumbs, kick digging,
brings to light sights buried inside
the smooth terrain of a locked up mind.

See a farmyard hen,
immortalised in print.
Baby books built with happy bright pictures,
chocolate cake sweet.
Little chicks drinking sun tickled water,
cleaner than often washed hands
of the fairy tale farmer,
honest provider scrubbing bloody palms.
"Out damn spot."

See a farmyard hen,
feathered and strong,
bolder than archaeopteryx,
now fattened until her legs buckle or break.
Trapped between bars by a hard boiled labourer.
Head shell tough, he does as he's paid.
See a childless mother's pain.
Her beak sawn off with a red, hot blade.
She can't stretch, peck or move in anyway,
locked away in barns,
locked away in minds.

See farmed hens,
together alone.
I can't be green as the fields where chickens don't roam.
No lush green distortion,
my bubble of blind buying could be burst
to stop her perpetually funded curse.

I could feel the joy of choosing to see
and not recharge this battery.

LOVELY FRUIT SALAD
for my family

Hey diddle dee!
One small blackberry.
Cook book map unearths treasure.
Veg marks the spot.
Ascend new tastes. My tongue, a flag
topping peaks of pumpkin pie.
Spinach smacked lips.
Peach smoothie sips.
Sunday's child pulls out a plum.
Different from other kids,
I jump over candle sticks.

Hi ho,
the derry-o,
discoveries to share.
She and me
. . . and broccoli.
Cracking corn like we just do care.
Juicy secrets of tangerine sunrise.
Bells in my head peel oranges and lemons.
Hearts tougher than cherry stones.
Together, our worries butternut squashed!
Soya Master.
Dandelion Dame.
Some wild fruits no one can tame.

Hickory dock.
2 veg in a wok.
But there's 3 in our home.
Not peas in a pod.
At first, he thinks we're chatting rhubarb.
"Rhubarb! Rhubarb! Rhubarb!"
She and me . . . and he won't see
the depths to quince and bean feast mince.

But food is much more than state of mind.
In a tasteless grown up world
it's a way we can find to unite and bind.

Scrambled Humpty's shell made whole.
3 mice turn, with sight restored,
snatch back their tails from farmers' wives.
Lamb slips free from Mary's crook.
Pussycat, pussycat spits at the Queen!
Ptu!
Spluttering monarch shrills *"Off with their heads!"*
but we're flowered up in our vegetable beds.

She and me . . . and he . . . agree.
It's okra, lentil, kiwi and grape!
Singing our ballad
of lovely fruit salad

and the cow jumps over the moon.

PULSE

for Ian

Pulse	beat.	Moth	heat.
Winged	horse.	Vein	deep.
Lub	dub.	Lub	dub.
Gee	hup.	Lift	feet.

Feet fly.	Eat high.	Raw or try to	bake / fry.
Make pie.	Wheat / rye.	Pulse beat, loud,	uncloud sky.
Take a bite	of fancy's flight.	Soar at quite	a hearty height.
Life of night.	Black light.	Stars like rice,	soul bright.

Leave no crumbs. Pulse beat drums. Motor hums.   2 up thumbs.
Big, full tums.   Best with chums. Can't do sums but breathe as one.
Joy comes.   Horse kick.   Healthy gums. Teeth click click.
House o' brick.   Pulse thick.   Tock tick.   Flax oil slick.

Quick to ground. Earth bound.   Un - wound.   Feet down.
Breath found.   All round.   Pulse pounds. A rooted sound.
Lub dub.   Lub dub.   No frown,   all loved up.
Winged horse.   Moth heat.   One pulse   strong beat.

Lub	dub.	Lub	dub.
No	frown, all	loved	up.
Broad	green	hearts	meet.
One	breath.	Pulse	deep.

I'M COMING OUT AS VEGAN!

Maybe not today.
I'm afraid.
Don't single me out from the pack.
Anything but that!
I'd love to be an ace, king, Jack the lad,
rugged and mean.
But no.
I know
I am a celery munching queen.

Sappy, soppy fruit.
Not a real butch man.
Can't change the hand I've been dealt.
It's limp.
Like water cress.
I confess I ravish radishes,
crave brussel sprout,

but I am a closet vegan
and I'm not coming out.

I've tried to be like those beef stocky guys raised on pork pies,
strutting to the beat of a deep battered drum stick.
Cocksure. Strident. Keep brains in their meat and two veg.
Big men. Big macs.
Sized super muscle flexing troopers.

I pretend I am like them.

Struggling home with shopping bags,
I've tried to hide my veggie mince.
Tried to look rough. Jerky tough.
Steak acting. Steak looking.
Tell me I am normal, I will sacrifice any lamb,

just tell me I am one of the gang
and not a gooseberry.
Anything but that.
So, my queer desires are kept under
lettuce wraps.

But like any iceberg, most of me's concealed.
I still secretly savour celeriac. Prefer asparagus to veal.
The only blood I suck's from orange. It sends me to nirvana.
In my bedroom under quilt unpeeling my banana.

Then, I chew open a new thought. Teeth slowly grind.
All this mastication almost made me blind.
It's here! Clear! Hits like lemon zest.
A cucumber coolness washes way all bitterness.
Tear up my cards! Grind them to pulp!
Gulp down fear with a sip of herbal tea.
Switch on the internet. Pull up m'trousers.
Google V E G A N M E N and find . . .
they're not all big girls' blouses!

But . . .
I . . .
AM!!

Yes! Check the mirror.
What a peachy fella.
This pumpkin's turned to Cinderella.
No feeble side salad, I'm the main dish!
Golden delish right to my core.
Olive skinned. Full of beans.
I'm coming out and proud.
Show those porkers I've got nuts!

Why'd I ever want to be part of their
cold, carnivorous crowd?

Real, butch men
or chickens
gauging gravied pie?
The truth, like onions, would make
most those lily livered boys cry.
They are macho as . . . nachos!
Strong? Virile? Quick?
How many of them could wring the neck of a little boy chick?
Or take a calf from its mother?
Or clip a piglet's teeth?
Seems these real men are icebergs too,
their truth hid deep beneath.

Overcome conditioning.
There is an inner voice.
I think it's normal to be caring.
I don't think compassion's a choice.
I think it's part of who I am,
like sex, like love, like skin.
This one small step took me so far!
Swapped fois gras for Mardi Gras!
My new taste buddies cheer *"Hurrah!"*
Let the party in!
Want the world to know.
Got to let it show.
"I'm coming!"

Pop my cherry!
Dance and shout.
I am vegan.
I'm coming out.

MY FAVOURITE MEALS

2008

My favourite meals come sudden,
speed of forest fire.
Sparks attack with whip crack.
Onions hitting the pan.
I never plan.
Think they make themselves.
Feels like my hands are guided,
controlled. It's magic,
like pyramid text or Ed Wood.

They tell me when friends are near
and something fills my fingers,
an unseen energy
cartwheels down from cupboards and cookbooks,
clatters awake my mind.

I don't mean dinner parties.
No chit-chat-trudging with a school friend's new wife.
Yawn swallowing through yarns of promotion,
their new car, clothes and
the taste of back patting that cheese grates my throat.

No. I mean dates with mates
and plates of pakora, crisp soft samosa,
soya ambrosia!
Fizzing drink flows and the air snogs your nose.
I know what my beans are for.
Stir fries. Bakes. Chocolate iced cakes.
My lasagne's style would make even Morrissey smile!
The sun shines out of my hoummous.

I don't mean that boastfully,
remember, it's the meals, not me,
I'm controlled. Bhajis ensnare
like Medusa's hair.

I've noticed how often other poets are there.
Their radars sense my oven glove's tiniest move.
Poets are always hungry.
As the steam clears they'll suddenly appear.
The real magic is having them there.
My favourite meals are the ones I share.

TOMORROW, I WILL GO DANCING

Today, I'm eating margarine straight from the tub
and I feel so guilty however hard I scrub.
My wrist's unbandaged, I'm trying not to rub
but I've so many sores that need lancing.
Tomorrow, I will go dancing.

My fingernails are rusty. Head's full of ills.
Chest hot and tender as stomach spills.
But tomorrow, I'm going to get these little pills.
See, everything about me needs enhancing.
Tomorrow, I will go dancing.

Tomorrow, you'll go dancing, in your glitter tat.
Absinthe! Vodka! You never get fat.
Laughing. Smiling. All that goes with that.
Today, I feel anxieties advancing.
Tomorrow, I will go dancing.

Hear my father's voice, warped and splintered today,
he says *"Misery will find you, boy, you'll never get away."*
My dick feels like a beehive on a warm, summer's day
when I see pretty things all preening and prancing.
Tomorrow, I will go dancing.

Everyone there's friendly. Falling into song.
I want to be loved. I've been lonely for so long.
Tomorrow is a vessel, sail way from all this wrong
where bitches say I'm ugly and can't sing.
Tomorrow, I will go dancing.

Today, I feel your laughter and it's gnawing in my head,
it is biting out the blisters where you burned until I bled,
if I panic . . . 'til I can't breathe, feel I'd be better dead,
well, I tell myself that risk is worth chancing.
Tomorrow, I will go dancing.

I want to join the happy crowds, glorious and glad.
I want to like pop music. Never feel bad.
My therapist's implying that I choose to be this sad.
I tell her, *"You know nothing . . . but if you're asking . . .*
I think she's asking?
She's asking.
Tomorrow, I will go dancing."

TRYING TO REMEMBER

I am trying to remember
there's a day that's going to be,
when I won't sit with silence sat
so clammy next to me.
I am trying to remember
there's a day that I will find.
It's beneath the swollen grin
of my slack window blind.

I am trying to remember
that one day I will go out.
I will push through the burly noise
that knocks the street about.
And I am trying to remember,
though this fact I'll have to check,
that you can go out here and not get
a knife in your neck.

My confidence is hungry
like my empty shelves.
I am trying to remember
bread and beans don't buy themselves.
Silence listens slowly,
chews skin around my thumb.
I am trying to remember
there's a day that's going to come

when I'll go back to the shop
and no longer see the knives
glinting in the check out girl
and lorry driver's eyes.
I am trying to remember
that I will feel safe, one day,
and yet, each night, it feels like
that day's getting further away.

BEERS IN YOUR BEDROOM
for Rachael K, for helping me save my life

We have beers in your bedroom.
My fears would be intoxicating without you.
Outside, car alarms shout at shadows,
a woman's scream stabs the night.

Inside, together
we are alive.
Your flat's above it all.
Door locked. Window open.
Glows from fag stubs, thin white dukes,
light a corkscrew path to morning.

Our tongues brighten dark.
These moments taste of unconcentrated truth,
Chaucer and tumblers of Fat Boy Slim.
We tape Woman's Hour to play backwards,
exchange identities under skin.
Hail bloody fairies and horns.

We dress up in old lovers' ideas,
hang ours up to dry, see what drips out first.
Dissect entrails of aborted stories.
Whole scripts wait in a typewriter's puckered spool
between shy, naked poems
printed only on sheets of dusk.

"Then, we unwrite the imperfect pop song.
Kurt Cobain and Kiki Dee sing
'Don't Go Breaking My Heart Shaped Box'."

Our nights are so heavy with talk
we might even . . . break through these floorboards,
crash into the spiked streets below,
so I cuddle your sentences. Grip tight.
Sit secure in our obscurity.

We're the extra features on a DVD
those with jobs are too busy to watch,
but we watch them and talk
ourselves down in thick blankets of sun.

Let us sleep through the violence of minutes and hours
that wage war against today's tired minds,
too burdened with action to slow down and think.
I drink to the courage
of these thoughtless grunts on the front line.
Raise my empty bottle.

We've drunk the night dry.
My voice lids won't keep open.
You wrap my words up warm.
Still, I know that they would freeze
out there
at bus stops, supermarket queues,
or sat, without vowels,
at office desks and the water cooler.

DO YOU SEE THIS NIGHT?

Do you see this night?
Towering, ancient
sour dream tree of petrified tears.
For years, this night
has blocked all hope of sunrise.
This night is solid wood

but I am going to break its branches.

This night's soiled roots
that have tugged so tight around my throat
are going to loosen . . .
are going to lose.

I've been bullied,
broke and aloned.
Now I'm blessed with restless passion.
Turn bruises into shields.
Like liquid metal I'm cooling my anger
into the greatest weapon.

   CRACK!

This night is splitting wood.

I am the axe against its bark,
bite like acid at the trunk.
With relentless vision,
eyes like machetes
and sweet strong pride, unshakeable.
My belief is unbreakable as I chop
chop
down
this
night.

   CRASH!

Unclog clear skies.
Breathe out my dreams.
Smell their freshly cut spices.
Taste their quivering nervous heat
as dust particles kiss the air.

This night is dead.
Felled.
Count the rings inside.
Each ring within its split core marks another year
I made it through.
I made it!
These rings are the rungs I've climbed
to find myself behind this night's silhouette.
I embrace the years I have conquered,
and will never fear the joy of ageing.

Joy of life without this night.
No longer telling myself
"I am weak."
Moon drowned words.
Shadow obscured sight.
I watered this night with my tears.

I wish . . . I could hold a fraction of the colour
that sparks and cracks inside me now
and convey it back through time,
back to when this night clung tightest
show myself,
"This night will end!"

Look around.
Already seeds of another night
are being sown at my feet.
A dark sapling claws at my ankle.
It is trying to take root.

THIS ROOM HAS LIPS / YOU SHOULD BE NAKED!
for Rod, these photos are for you

This room has lips.
They pucker to the beat,
x ‿ x ‿ x ⌒ x ‿ x
A glitter smeared kiss
warm as lover's sweat.
These dim-lit walls are open mouthed,
bricks salivating,
smacking molten honey.

The mirrorball drools light.

We dance,
wet, as fresh varnished nails,
sticky blotches on sin blessed skin.
Hallowed be the flame,
Halloween be thy name,
a fiery tongue that licks the flesh,
caresses unwrapped chest.

We dance
in lines, like bright, jagged teeth,
grinding together,
solid sharp.
Eyes glisten like newly drilled fillings.
This room has had a feast of sweet treats.

Now, it whispers
lies
with hot, treacherous lips,
sweeter than a shared alcopop.
"Dominic . . . Morning will not come."

I want to be drunk,
sucked through a straw, eyes first,
absorbed and digested into this room.
Don't spit me out.

Clamp your jaw hard on my leg.
Don't send me home.
Grip me here where I feel tasty,
have a chance of being swallowed.

You should be naked!
Tugged. Stripped
to your radiance.
You are raw.
Stark. Pure
electrifying skin.
Interstellar.
Moral melting wonder.
Ultra violent heat.
I am your satellite,
satellite of lust.
Rip out of your clothes.
Shine!

Burn through this vacuum of fabric.
Tear those hollows of textile.
Free your fire smacked nudity,
soft magnetic curves.

Your natural beauty's eclipsed
by eternal night of denim.
Nipples chaff on cold cotton.
Concealed thighs secretly shake,
nuclearly fused,
aching to break!
I know your supernova quakes
beneath an airless gulf of cloth.

Touch me

and body hair prickles upright.
Tiny bursts of solar flare
trying to penetrate
the dark fibre space in between us.

76

WE TRAVEL

We travel.
Your Step Dad is stranded.
Your Step Dad's a castle,
thinks he's strong, defiant,
vats of burning oil high on his battlements.
He'd keep us hidden.
Sh!
Hush hush!
Locked in violet shame.
From portcullis he threatens spears and broadswords.
He's from another time.
We see him crumbling. Ancient ruin
hacking the ropes of his mind rotten drawbridge.
"Protect the gentry! Keep out foreigners!"
We're long gone.

We travel.
Our world is moving on without him.
Flying carpet over breath giving views.
Landscapes unfold light in our lungs.
Broadens our chests. Room for more medals.
Your Step Dad's proof of how we've earned them!

We travel.
Breathe deep futures.
Longer nights,
open hips bumping in funky hot club air.
Cold evenings, linking toes.
Warm mornings, swallowed in bed,
We rise like cake,
freshly baked,
raw cane and syrup.
There's a photo of us in a place we've yet to be.

It's on the last shot of my camera,
the one I've still not taken,
I'm saving it for you.
But let's not rush.
I am in love with the journey.
I am in love with you.

We travel together
through ideas yet unknown.
Excitement singes the tips of our brains.
Feasting on experience.
Heavy with joy.
We're greedy!
Gluttons for pleasure.
Trying to eat back the years we were starved of attention,
judged for affection,
a guilty secret made out of our simple intention.

To love.

We travel with glory.
Your Step Dad shrinks outside our airplane window.
Huffing, puffing wolf with no pigs.
He lives in a fairy tale, brick houses everywhere.
We sail in a jack-o'-lantern way after midnight.
The kid in us is still alive!
Racing forward through unexplored lands.
Slaying dragons with sticks and stones.

THE ROAD TO TREFASSER (PART 2)

Below brick.
Under voices.
Beneath chemical coats and straps of road.
This land is naked.
Magic.

No number of dusks and dawns can age its innocence.
Like a child in ill fitting uniform,
forced into lessons it takes a lifetime to forget,
this land just wants to strip off,
streak bare-arsed cheeky round the sun
and skinny dip in the sky's deep end
where it's dark enough to see stars.

We try to be friends.
Humbly share with lambs and beetles,
baby peregrines, tucked up in cliff beds,
swallows swooping beside Rod's car.
Gabble of beast, gossip of bugs and
Louie
carefully mapping mornings with gentle orange paws,
trying to track the sunniest napping spot today.
Louie is no cat.
He is our Ginger Prince of Strumble Head.

Rod reads us poems. Mum's making nut roast nuttier.
Her cottage warm with words and laughter.

After dinner, we'll walk to the pebble beach,
see this land still nearly nude.
A vast wild-calm across pink, purpled fields
where, embracing rock and sea,
witches dance.

SITS WITH BUDDLEIA

A man's hands click fit
in puzzle of plant.
His solution.
He's not clumsy here.
Fingers earth brush
as the land paints him.

Foxgloves pattern his hands
far from office men's acrid chatter.
They want things nice for a visit.
Think they own the daisies.
Say this land needs weeding.

He clears the stage
for roses to work their confident flourish
in theatres without seats.
Their best shows need no audience.
Bluebells fill empty country homes
with Judy Garlands of applause,
warm as a beckoning kettle.

He grows in sunshine.
Meets a hot mug of tea
with a hundred types of biscuit.
Sits with buddleia.
Sips and dunks.
Here he is.

OUTRODUCTION

Thanks for reading my lovely fruity book. I hope it filled you with lovely fruity whoosh.

I resisted an urge at the start to write some Lou Reed-esque demand, "Read this book start to finish in one go without a single toilet break", though at first I was keen for this selection to be seen as one poetic novel. Now it's all done, I think it's nice to take a more Dr Who approach. I don't own these moments. Dip in my time-line however you fancy.

I will say this, next time you dip in, these words go very well with a big slice of cake. I think most things do. Here is a recipe I particularly enjoy:

> Take a cup and a half of flour,
> three quarters of a cup of sugar,
> three quarters of a cup of soya milk,
> one quarter of a cup of oil,
> a couple of teaspoons of vanilla essence,
> one vegan egg replacer (from your local health
>   food shop)
> and your favourite fruity jam.

Set oven for 180 degrees centigrade.
In a big bowl, pour the flour and sugar.
Add soya, oil, vanilla and egg replacer.
Gently mix.
Divide between two grease proof trays and cook
    for 15 minutes.
When its done, leave 'til cool before taking them
    out their trays.
Spread your favourite fruity jam on one half.
Pop the other half on top.
Huzzah!

Cake, poetry and dancing with the ones you love. Can't think of anything more beautiful.

Wishing you peace and glitter smeared kisses,

Dominic ✖